Made in the USA
Monee, IL
11 August 2021

75477937R00066